MAP YOUR PLANET

NATURAL RESOURCES

ANNABEL SAVERY

Cavendish Square

Published in 2024 by Cavendish Square Publishing, LLC
2544 Clinton Street, Buffalo, NY 14224

Website: cavendishsq.com

Editor: Annabel Savery
Designer: Clare Nicholas
Series designer: Rocket Design (East Anglia) Ltd

The publisher would like to thank the following for permission to reproduce their pictures:
Getty: ClaraNila 3(background) & 19(t), Olgaviare 4, slavemotion 5(c), Andrei Stanescu 6(b), InkkStudios 7(t), Beyondwonder 8(cl), Ankur Vishnoi 8(b), mazzzur 9(t), SB Stock 9(b), guenterguni 10(b), ArtistGNDphotography 11, kruwt 12(cl), ahavelaar 13(t), Darinburt 14(b), georgeclerk 15(c), Philips 15(cr), LuCaAr 16(b), BeyondImages 17(t), RomanBabakin 17(b), Florent MARTIN 18(t), HAYKIRDI 18(b), Juan Jose Napuri 19(br), Pavliha 21(c), Pavliha 21(b), meliusphotography 23(t), ymgerman 23(b), Plamen Galabov 24–25(ct), typhoonski 24(b), miroslav_1 25(c), Cn0ra 27(c), Blue Planet Studio 26, Cristian Lourenço 28(b), Sjo 29(t), JarnoVerdonk 29(b); NASA: 12(bl), 20(cl); Our World In Data: 15(b), 27(b); Shutterstock: Yuriy Kulik fc(r) & 1(r), Sean Hsu fc(l) & 1(l), Frontpage 5(t), VectorMine 6(t), Designua 7(c), marico design 14(t), wjarek 16(cr), NoPainNoGain 19(bl), Vecton 26(t), BlueRingMedia 27(t), snapgalleria 28(cr).
Design elements from Shutterstock.
Map illustrations: Julian Baker: 8–9, 13, 17, 20–21, 25, 29.

Cataloging-in-Publication Data

Names: Savery, Annabel.
Title: Natural resources / Annabel Savery.
Description: New York : Cavendish Square Publishing, 2024. | Series: Map your planet | Includes glossary and index.
Identifiers: ISBN 9781502668530 (pbk.) | ISBN 9781502668547 (library bound) | ISBN 9781502668554 (ebook)
Subjects: LCSH: Natural resources--Juvenile literature. | Conservation of natural resources--Juvenile literature.
Classification: LCC HC85.S28 2024 | DDC 333.7--dc23

CPSIA compliance information: Batch #CSCSQ24:
For further information contact Cavendish Square Publishing LLC at 1-877-980-4450.

Printed in the United States of America

Find us on

CONTENTS

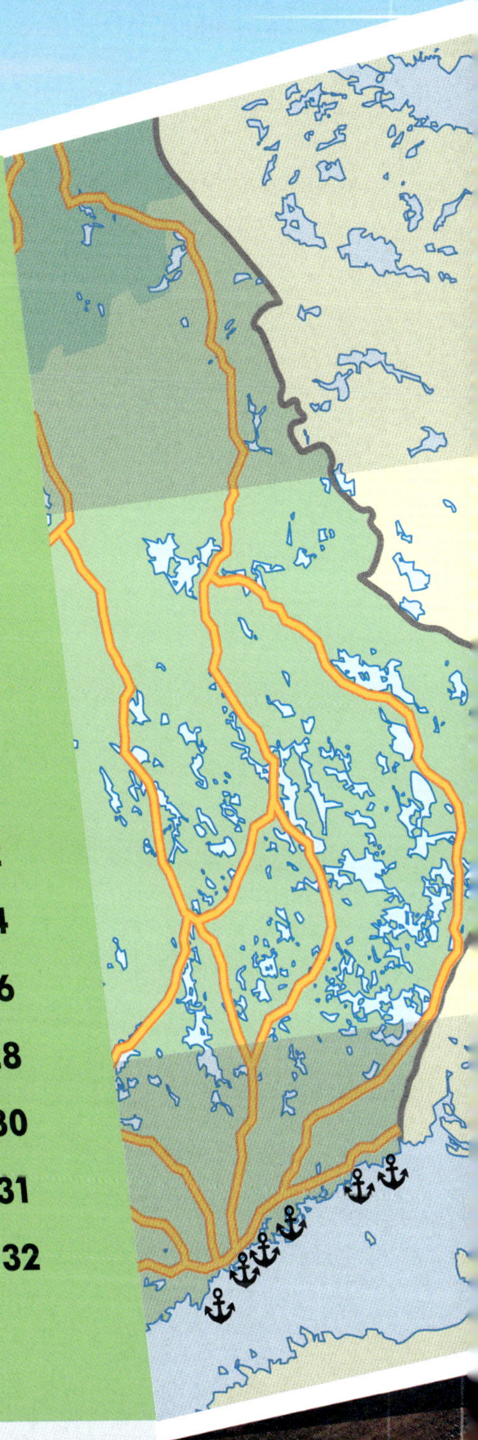

EARTH'S RESOURCES

Natural resources come from the world around us. Think of the water you drink and wash with, the food that you eat, how your television is powered, and the house you live in. How often do you think about where these things come from?

RENEWABLES AND NONRENEWABLES

Resources are divided into two categories. Renewable resources are those that will continue to reproduce, such as wood, animals, or plants. Resources such as sunlight, wind, and water are all classed as renewable, too. Nonrenewable resources are found in the Earth's crust and are limited. These include minerals, oil, coal, and natural gas. Once these are used up, there won't be any more.

Marble is a type of hard rock. It can be mined in huge blocks for use in building or sculpture, or crushed into stone for making roads and foundations. It is a nonrenewable resource that has taken millions of years to form.

DIRECT AND INDIRECT

Humans use the planet's resources both directly and indirectly. We chop down wood for houses, mine stone for building, and fish for food. This is direct use. Using resources indirectly means that we benefit from the things that they do naturally. Trees clean the air and their roots hold land in place, preventing erosion and flooding. Natural resources must be used and managed carefully. If those we use indirectly are damaged or used up, we will permanently damage the environment we depend on.

Brazil has some of the largest areas of rain forest in the world but much of the forest is being cut down to make way for farmland. This removes trees that clean our air.

MAP MASTERS

In the past, scientists made maps by going out on foot and recording land features, or using photographs taken from planes. Today, satellites help scientists to study the Earth and monitor the use of resources.

Satellites orbit high above the Earth and take photographs of the surface.

The population on Earth is now so vast that some of the world's resources are being stretched to the breaking point.

A WORLD OF WATER

Looking around you, it might seem like water is everywhere – especially when it rains! But how much water actually is there? Water covers 71 percent of the Earth's surface, but most of this is either salty seawater or locked up in glaciers. So how do we find freshwater to use?

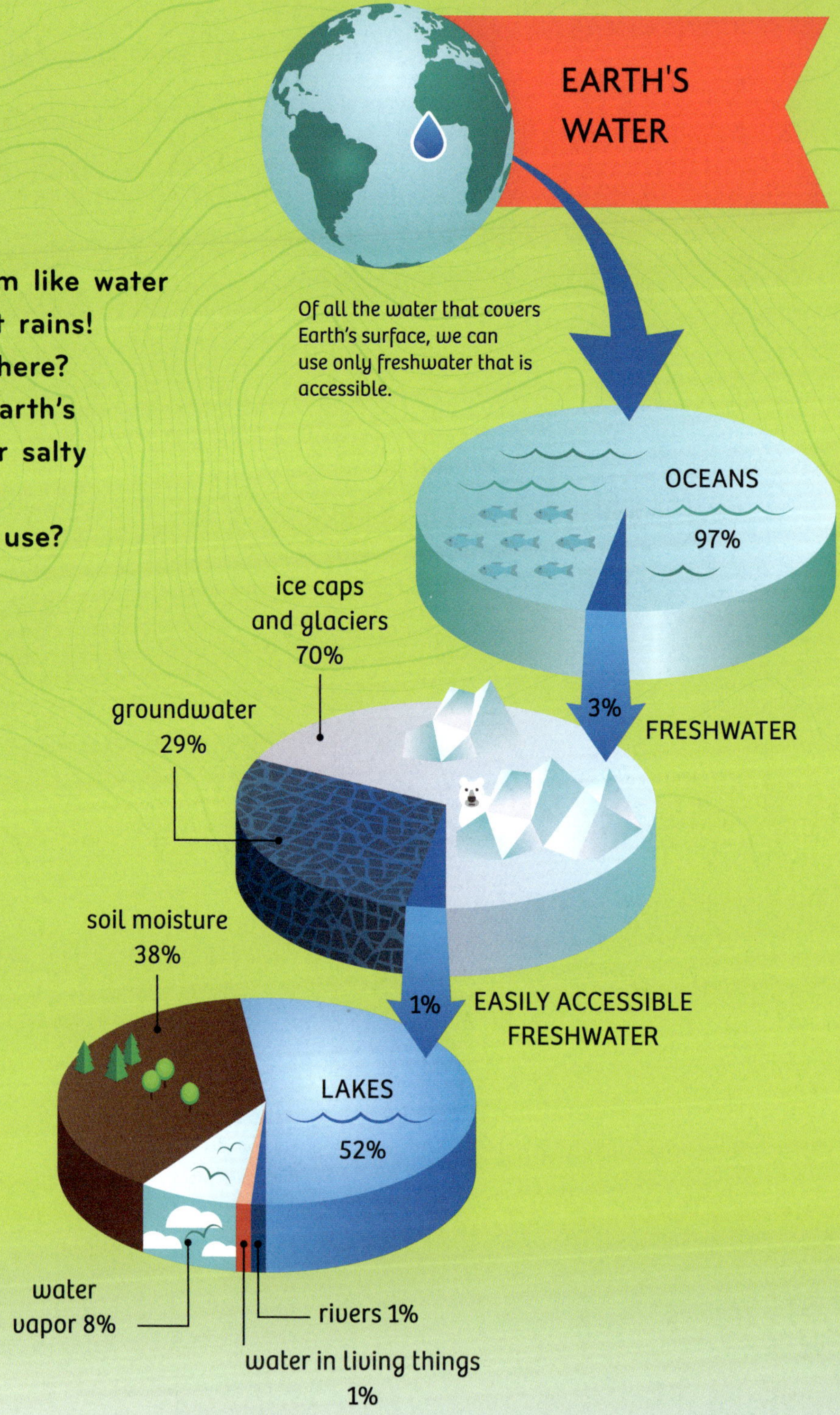

THE WATER WE USE

Water can be taken from rivers, lakes, and reservoirs, or it can be pumped up from under the ground. Next, it needs to be cleaned to make it safe to use before being pumped into our homes. Once used, water must be cleaned again before going back into natural water systems.

The California Aqueduct System pushes water over the Tehachapi Mountains to supply Southern California!

HOW WE USE WATER

Humans use an incredible amount of water every day. Washing your hands, using the toilet, and washing clothes all use water. It is also used in farming to water crops and feed animals. Energy production uses water and so does clothes and car manufacturing. The problem is that water is not always looked after. Waste and chemicals are polluting our water sources, causing problems both for nature and people.

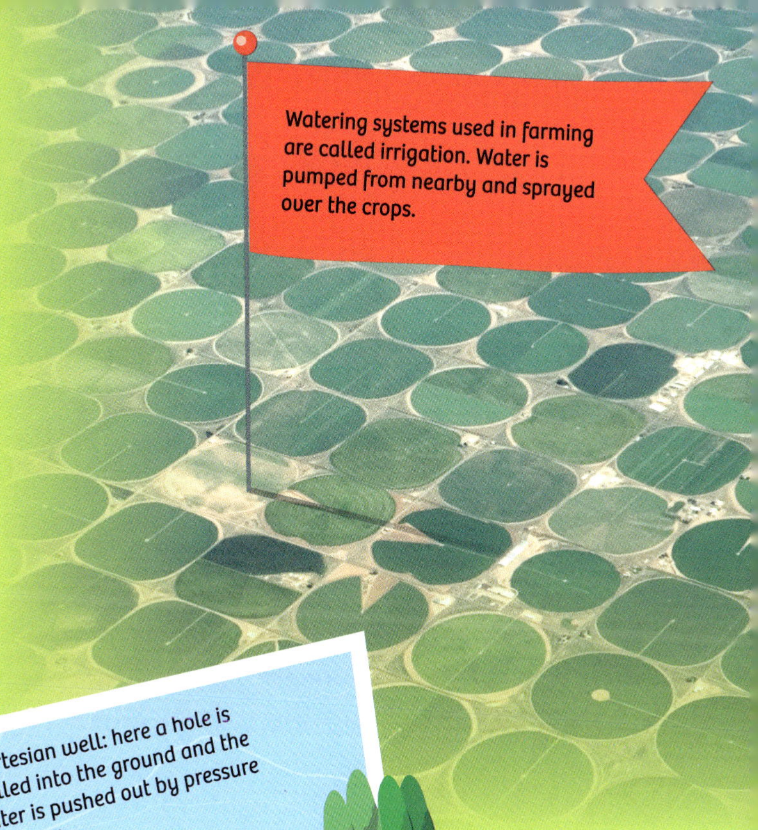

Watering systems used in farming are called irrigation. Water is pumped from nearby and sprayed over the crops.

MAP MASTERS

Water stored underground is called groundwater. Rain and snow seep into the ground and water is then stored in cracks and holes in the rock. Groundwater must be pumped to the surface from a well. Scientists find groundwater by looking at the surface for springs or water-loving plants. They also look at the types of rock to see which might hold water underground.

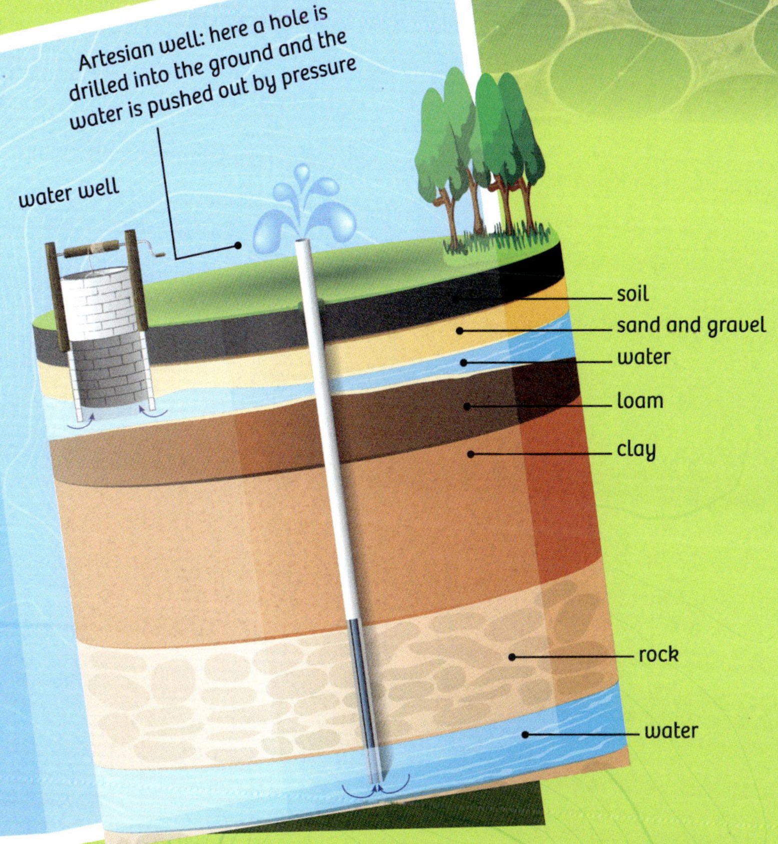

WATER CONSUMED DURING PRODUCTION

MAPPING THE GANGES RIVER

The great Ganges River supplies freshwater to a population of around 400 million people in northern India. It is a vital water source, but it has suffered so much from pollution that it is fast becoming a danger to the people who depend on it.

THE GREAT GANGES

The source of the Ganges is high in the Himalaya Mountains. Crystal-clear streams trickle from the Gangotri glacier, feeding streams that become the Ganges. Smaller rivers join the Ganges as it flows through the land all the way to the great delta, where it empties into the Bay of Bengal.

1 SETTLEMENTS

Many towns and cities have been built along the Ganges and the rivers that flow into it: Agra, Lucknow, Allahabad, Varanasi, Kolkata, and many more. The river provides freshwater to the towns and cities it flows through, but it also collects pollution.

2 WATERING CROPS

Over time, sediment carried down from the mountains has created rich farming lands around the river. Since the 4th century BCE, canal systems have been used to bring water to crops.

3 VARANASI

The Ganges River is worshipped by the Hindu religion as Ganga Mata or Mother Ganga. Along the river are places of holy importance and sites of pilgrimage.

Despite its importance to the people of India, the Ganges has become highly polluted. Human waste, litter, and chemicals from industry and farming all pour into the Ganges. This makes it dangerous both to humans and animal life.

LIVING OFF THE LAND

While you are out walking, do you think of the land beneath your feet as a resource? Land is used for growing food crops – everything from tea to beans; raising animals, such as cows, sheep, pigs, or chickens; and also growing crops for textiles, such as cotton.

FARMING THROUGH TIME

The first humans were nomadic, moving to find new food sources. Over time, people began to settle and learned how to grow crops and raise animals. As civilizations grew, they discovered ways of increasing the amount of food they could produce. Today most farms are commercial, growing and selling large amounts to feed the world's huge population. Land has now become an important and valuable resource.

Farmers plant rice by hand in a paddy field in Vietnam.

SCIENCE AND FARMING

The science of farming began with early civilizations using crop rotation, a system of changing which crops are grown in each field each year, and irrigation, a system of bringing water into farmland. Since then, machines, chemical pesticides, and fertilizers have all been invented to boost crop production. Unfortunately, many inventions have brought pollution and other problems. Scientists are looking for ways to produce crops without exhausting the land and water sources, or using harmful chemicals.

THE CHALLENGE

Somehow, we must increase food production while also trying to take care of the environment. Confusingly, an enormous amount of the food produced today, nearly one-third, goes to waste.

MAP MASTERS

It is always good to know where your food comes from. The system of food miles is a great way to track how far a food item has come from its original growing source to your plate.

A New Zealand-grown apple eaten in the UK has traveled about 11,687 miles (18,809 km).

A Costa Rican banana travels 5,789 miles (9,317 km) to be eaten in Switzerland.

MAPPING THE NETHERLANDS

Welcome to the Netherlands, a European country known for its waterways, windmills, and tulips. It is small and highly populated, and yet it is the second biggest exporter of food in the world. The only country ahead of it is the U.S., a country with 270 times its landmass!

PRECISION FARMING

More than half the land in the Netherlands is used for agriculture. The country's top exports are vegetables and vegetable seed. Some Dutch farmers have turned to new technology to increase quantity while also reducing the use of pesticides and fertilizers, and antibiotics for livestock.

1 MAKING NEW LAND

Many areas of land in the Netherlands have been reclaimed from the sea, including the Westland area. They have used a system of polders: using dikes to block off the sea and pumps to drain the area. The Flevoland region was created in this way.

2 GREENHOUSE GROWING

The region of Westland in the Netherlands is home to vast greenhouses. Greenhouse farming allows farmers to control the light and temperature, creating good growing conditions all the time. As with any new method, there may be a downside. Greenhouses do not allow for natural ecosystems and biodiversity. Lighting the greenhouses can cause light pollution, creating problems for nighttime creatures.

3 TECHNOLOGY TIME

Wageningen is home to one of the biggest agricultural universities. Around it is an area known as "Food Valley" where many new technologies are tested. Hi-tech equipment allows farmers to monitor precisely the levels of water and nutrients in the soil, and the growth of each plant. Technology on some farms can include remote vehicles and quadcopter drones!

The Netherlands began to focus on food production at the end of World War II when the country experienced extreme food shortages and many lost their lives.

The Oostersheldekering dam is part of the Delta Works. In 1953, a huge North Sea storm surge flooded the southwest region. The Delta Works project built a series of storm defenses to make sure it would never happen again.

WOODLAND WONDERLAND

Wood is all around us. We use it for paper, furniture, houses, fences, bridges, and more. It is also one of the most valuable indirect resources we have. Trees take the harmful carbon dioxide out of the air and give out oxygen, and forests provide habitats essential to the world's biodiversity.

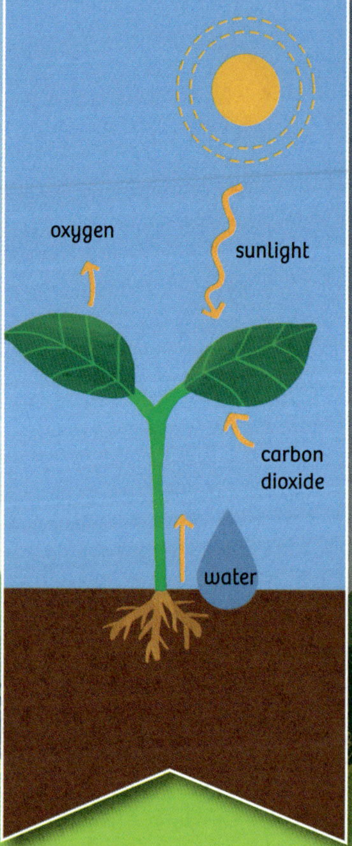

THE LOGGING INDUSTRY

Many people around the world depend on the logging and timber industries for their livelihoods. These industries include cutting trees down, transporting and processing them into smaller timber for building and furniture, and making pulp for papermaking. Clear cutting is a process in which every tree is felled and cleared away. This is often done to make way for the land to be used for farming. Selective logging takes out specific trees, but the forest can still be damaged by felling and machinery moving through woodland.

Logging in the Pacific Northwest region of the United States began in the 1820s. Today, plans are in place to protect land and wildlife.

TIME TO GROW

Silviculture means taking care of woodland to make sure it can keep growing healthily. Trees grow slowly and need space, good soil, and water. As well as human activity, threats to forests include fire and pests. Although trees are classed as a renewable resource, it takes time and space to replant trees and allow them to grow.

Many systems are now in place to manage woodland and protect the world's forests.

Although forest fires can be natural events that are part of a life cycle, in recent years some have raged dangerously out of control. Some scientists think this is due to climate change.

This map shows what percentage of each country is covered in established forest.

MAP MASTERS

Forests cover around 30 percent of the world. However, woodland is not evenly distributed. Some countries are very thickly forested, and some have vast forested areas. China, Russia, the U.S., Canada, and Brazil have the largest expanses of forest.

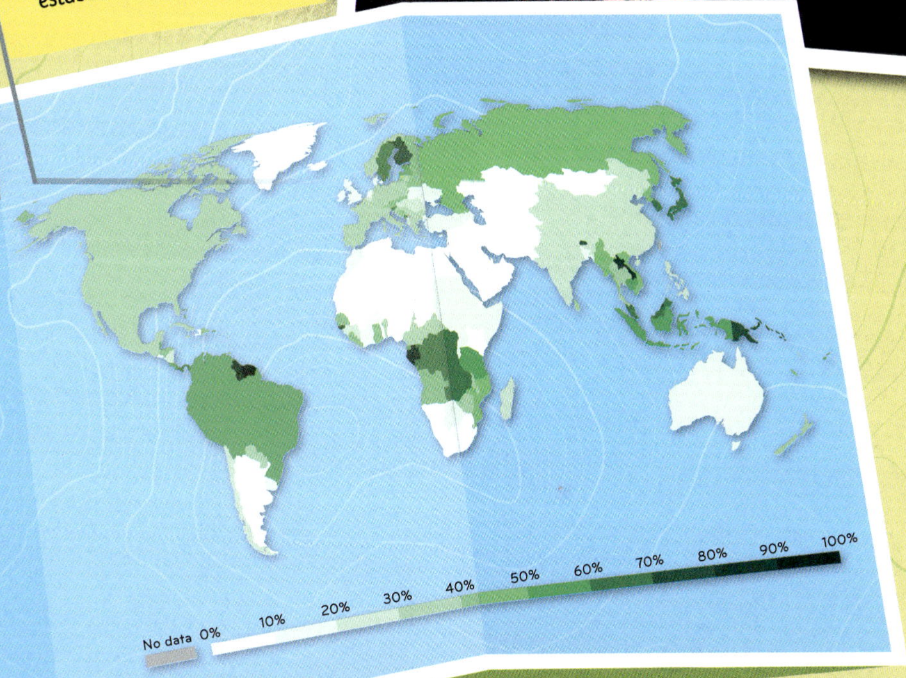

MAPPING FINLAND'S FORESTS

Finland is one of the world's top wood producers. Over 70 percent of the country is wooded and the country has done a lot to protect this valuable resource.

SLOW GROW

Finland's forests are sustainably managed. This means foresters aim to let more wood grow per year than the amount they cut down. They make sure the forests remain a renewable resource by managing their use. A short growing season means that Finland's trees grow slowly, leading to high-value wood.

1 NORTHERN FOREST

Finland's forests form part of the northern coniferous forest belt, which covers land in the northern hemisphere: from Alaska, through Siberia, to the far east of Russia. Finland's northernmost forested places are Utsjoki and Enontekiö.

2 PROTECTED ZONES

Around 12 percent of Finland's forests are protected from the logging industry. This preserves the area's biodiversity and allows animals, such as bears, elk, wolves, and lynx, to live there.

The country has over 15 seaports that are used for exporting and importing.

3 MOVING TIMBER

Transportation is a big concern for the forestry industry. Wood is a heavy product requiring big trucks, but transport must be done without damaging the land.

4 SEASONS

In the far north, the winter can last 200 days, leaving around 100 days for the warmer growing season. This season is longer in the southern regions of the country.

Many people in Finland rely on the timber industry. It employs 42,000 people directly and there are many more businesses that are linked with it.

MINERAL MINING

Ancient humans first began mining in prehistoric times, when they made tools and sharp-edged weapons from a rock called flint. Later, gold, copper, and silver were discovered in riverbeds. In time, people began to seek out particular types of stone for building.

The great pyramids at Giza in Egypt are one of the earliest examples of people mining stone for building.

WHAT ARE MINERALS?

Mining means digging a hole in the Earth to take out valuable rock and minerals. Minerals are substances found in the Earth's crust. They are inorganic, meaning they are not made from plant matter. Minerals can be metallic, such as iron, copper, gold, and silver. Some metals are found in their pure form, others are found mixed up in rocks and need to be extracted. Rocks containing metallic minerals are called ores. Minerals can also be nonmetallic. These include salt, sulfur, and gemstones.

This is a salt cave in Turkey. Salt deposits are created from seas that have dried up over thousands of years and become buried.

The enormous Fimiston gold mine in Western Australia is known as the Super Pit – it is one of the biggest in the world.

MINING TODAY

Today mining is an enormous industry. The most mined minerals are iron, bauxite (aluminium ore), phosphate rock (used to make fertilizers and calcium), and gypsum (used to make plaster and fertilizers). Different minerals need different types of mines, depending on where they are found in the Earth's crust. Open-pit mines are vast holes scraped in the Earth's surface. Tunnel mines dig deep, narrow holes to find substances far belowground. There are many environmental issues caused by the mining industry: disrupting ecosystems and chemical pollution of the air and waterways are just two.

MAP MASTERS

Prospecting means looking for minerals to mine. Once prospecting relied on simply looking at the landscape. Prospectors would look at the colors of rock as a clue to what might be beneath them. They would dig in the ground and swirl muddy sediment from riverbeds to see what it contained. These practices are all still done today – but with a lot more science and technology to help make findings more accurate.

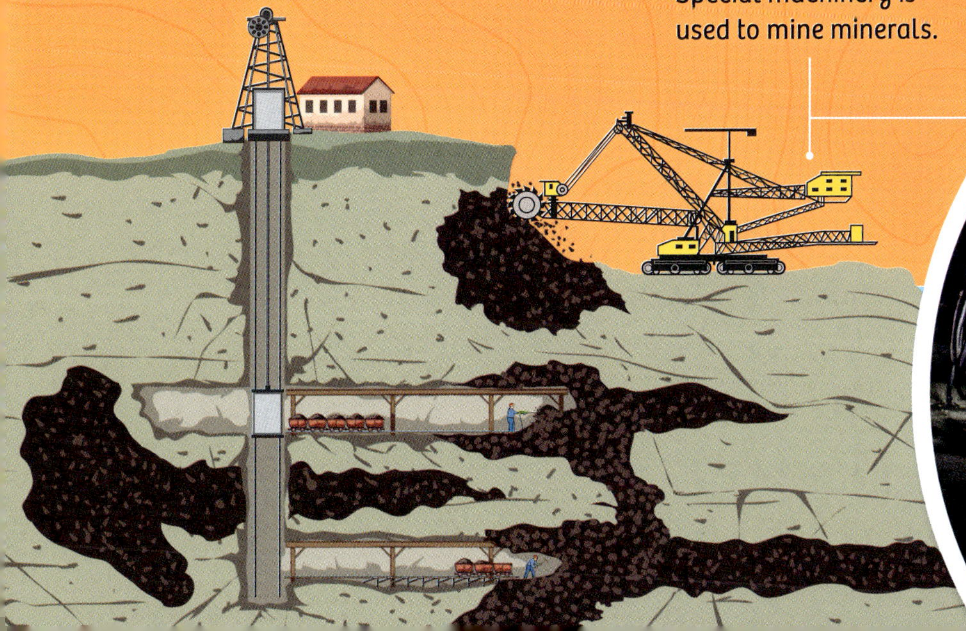

Special machinery is used to mine minerals.

MAPPING
BINGHAM CANYON MINE

Nestled in the Oquirrh mountain range near Salt Lake City, Utah, is the world's biggest human-made excavation. It is so big it can be seen from space.

UTAH'S BIGGEST MINE

The Bingham Canyon mine is a vast open-pit copper mine. It is 2.5 miles (4 km) wide, and over 0.6 mile (1 km) deep! The mine produces copper, molybdenum (a mineral used to combine with other metals), gold, and silver.

FACT

MINERALS HAVE BEEN MINED HERE FOR OVER 100 YEARS. THE MINE'S TOTAL HISTORICAL PRODUCTION VALUE IS $174 BILLION!

1 HI-TECH MINE

The mine has a 5-mile (8 km) conveyor system to move rock from the pit to the processing plant at Copperton. The pit uses global satellite navigation systems to position its drills.

2 GOING GREEN

Owners of the mine have begun a substantial cleanup program, aiming to repair some of the environmental damage of the past and operate efficiently today. They have closed their own coal power plant, near Magna, and switched to using green energy. Much of the equipment they use is electric and low-emission technology, and they have sought to restore ecosystems in the surrounding area.

3 LANDSLIDE

On April 10, 2013, two massive landslides shook 160 million tons (145 million tonnes) of waste rock into the bottom of the mine. Thankfully, no one was injured. The company had sensitive radar systems in place that could detect changes in the pit walls. They were able to predict the slide and evacuate the mine.

FOSSIL FUELS

Fossil fuels are part of our everyday life. The majority of power comes from fossil fuel energy; cars run on fossil fuel, homes are heated with oil, and countless products are made from by-products of the petroleum industry. It really is everywhere!

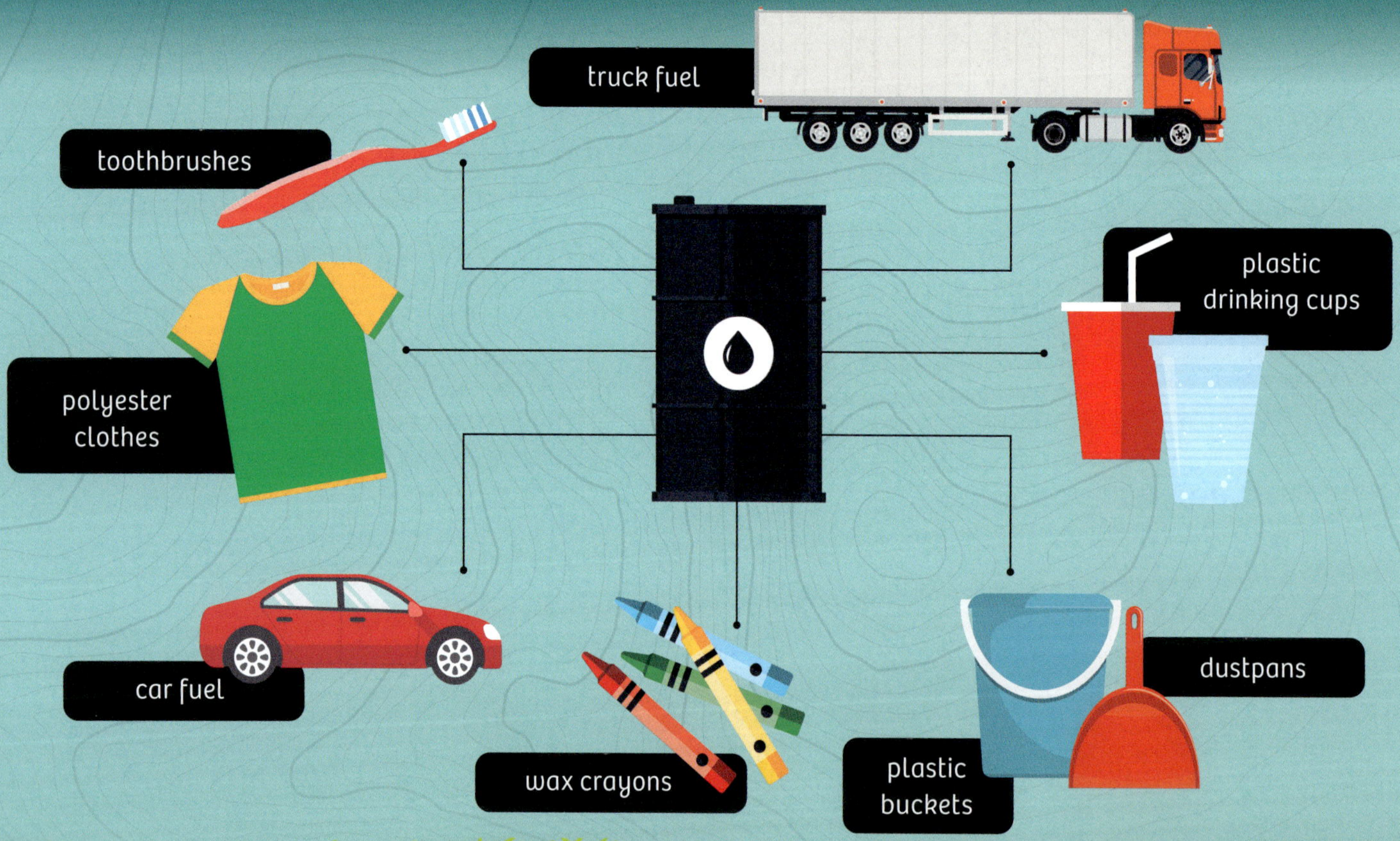

TAKE YOUR TIME

Over millions of years, small organisms, plants, and animals have become buried in the earth. With high heat and pressure deep belowground, this organic matter has changed into oil, coal, and natural gas. The long time it takes for these fossil fuels to form means they are nonrenewable. When they are gone, that's it!

GET DIGGING

To be used, fossil fuels must first be extracted from the ground. Coal can be found both close to the Earth's surface and deep below it. It is mined using strip mines or deep pit mines. To extract oil or natural gas, miners drill deep into the Earth's crust and pump it out.

In longwall coal mining, a machine called a shearer slices along a wall of coal to break it up, ready for extraction.

GLOBAL WARMING

Fossil fuel use is damaging our planet. To be used as fuel, fossil fuels are burned. Burning them produces large amounts of polluting gases. When released into the air, these gases build up in the atmosphere, trapping heat from the sun and warming the planet. This is known as global warming and is causing the climate around the world to change, damaging vital resources and ecosystems.

At a coal-fired power station, burning coal heats water to produce steam. The steam turns turbines to generate power. The steam is then cooled in tall towers and the water can be used again.

MAP MASTERS

We know that there is a limit to the amount of fossil fuels in the Earth. Scientists try to work out how long the reserves will last. Most say around 50 years, depending on how we use them.

The U.S. has the greatest coal reserves, the Middle East countries have the greatest oil reserves, and Russia has the greatest reserves of natural gas.

MAPPING THE MIDDLE EAST OIL FIELDS

An area in the Middle East known as the Arabian–Iranian Basin holds vast oil reserves.

OIL REFINING

The oil pumped up from below the Earth's crust is known as crude oil. It is not very useful in its raw form, so it needs to be refined. Oil refineries can be enormous – some the size of small cities. They are often built near rivers or the sea as they use a lot of water.

1 OIL FIELDS

There are spaces in the Earth's crust where oil has collected. These are known as oil fields. The biggest oil fields are called giant and supergiant fields. Supergiant fields can hold as much as 1 billion barrels of oil.

2 PIPE TIME

Oil wells are often some distance from refineries. Pipelines are used to transport oil from wells to refineries, ports, or storage areas. Smaller oil fields use tanker trucks instead of pipelines.

TANKER SHIPS

Oil can also be transported in tanker ships across the ocean. Supertankers can hold as much as 2 million barrels. Past disasters have led to new designs of tankers – the double hull should prevent oil spills if the tanker were to run aground.

Oil was used in many ways by ancient civilizations. They found places where it naturally rose to the ground in "seeps".

FACT

THE ARABIAN-IRANIAN BASIN HOLDS MORE THAN 20 SUPERGIANT FIELDS!

CLEAN RESOURCES

Replacing fossil fuel use with clean energy sources and natural products is vital to the future of our planet. Solar, wind, hydro, geothermal, tidal, and biomass are all forms of renewable energy.

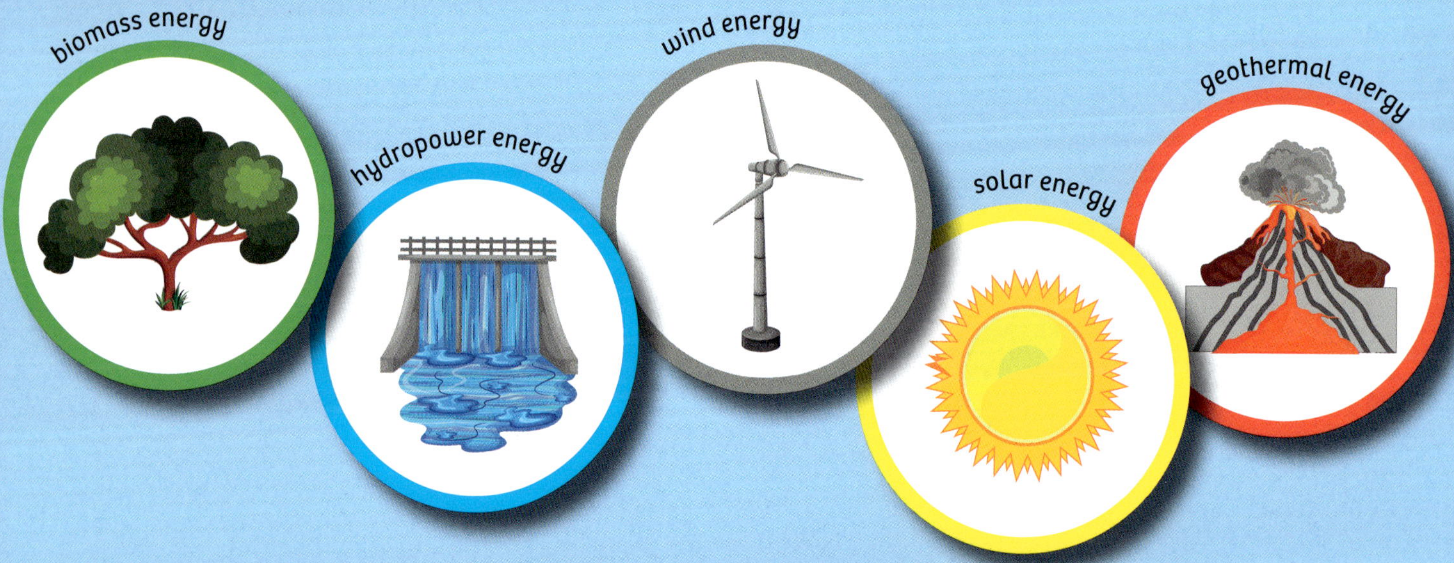

SOLAR POWER

Solar panels collect the sun's rays and turn it into energy. Panels vary in size from small to vast! While this is clean energy, it takes a lot of space to produce large amounts of power, sunlight is not constant, and the materials used to make solar panels can be toxic.

Solar and wind technologies are developing all the time. Currently, it takes a lot of turbines and solar panels to produce the same amount of energy as fossil fuels.

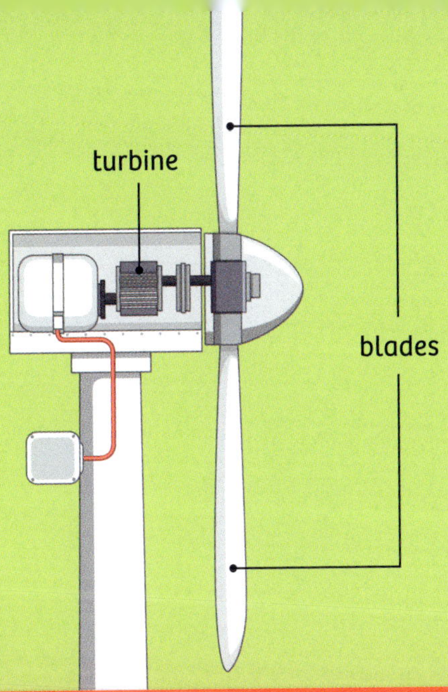

WIND POWER

To generate energy from wind, you need a wind turbine. As the blades turn in the wind, they turn the turbine to make power. Wind turbines are placed on hills or out at sea to catch the strongest winds. Building these enormous machines is expensive and takes a lot of materials. Wind turbines can also be noisy, which affects wildlife and people living nearby.

THE PLASTIC PROBLEM

It is not only in energy that people are looking for clean, green solutions. Plastic is one of the world's biggest problems and is a by-product of the oil industry. Chemicals are another problem as they find their way into our water sources. Increasingly, people are looking for plastic- and chemical-free products to replace those they use every day.

MAP MASTERS

If you live in a high-income country, it's easy to take power for granted. It works with the flick of a switch and you don't have to think about it. However, 13 percent of people in the world do not have access to electricity – this is 940 million people. The majority are in sub-Saharan Africa.

Countries classed as high-income are assumed to have 100% household electricity.

MAPPING THE ITAIPÚ DAM

The big rivers that charge through the landscape of Brazil hold huge potential for generating power. Today, two-thirds of Brazil's power comes from hydropower, and one of the main sources is the Itaipú Dam on the Paraná River.

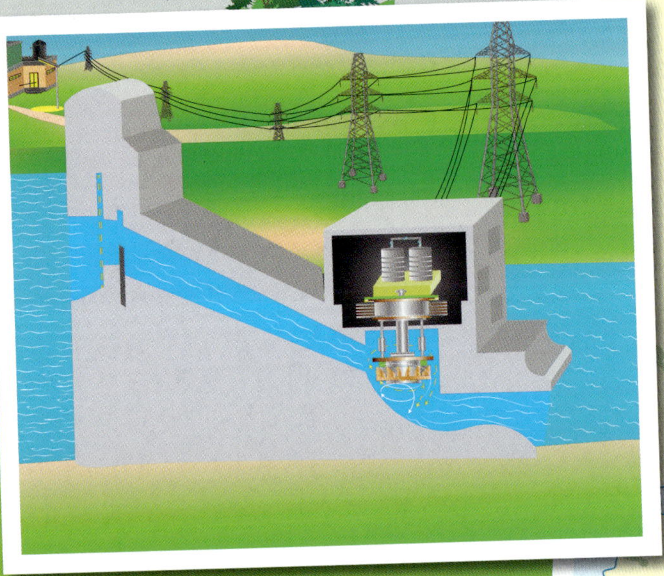

BUILDING DAMS

To generate energy using hydropower you need to create a dam. This is a large wall that holds back a body of water. The water is then let through turbines in the wall. The water turns the turbines and energy is created.

The Itaipú Dam sits on the border of Brazil and Paraguay. It is a joint project between the two countries. It took seven years to build and is nearly 657 feet (200 m) high.

Below the reservoir are the Guairá Falls – once an incredible spectacle.

1 BUILDING WORK

To construct the dam, engineers had to change the flow of the Paraná River by building a barrier. After creating the dam, they took the barrier down, allowing the river to flood a large area and create a reservoir. To the north of the dam the reservoir stretches for about 100 miles (160 km). Allowing an area to flood is a complicated decision that affects both people and wildlife.

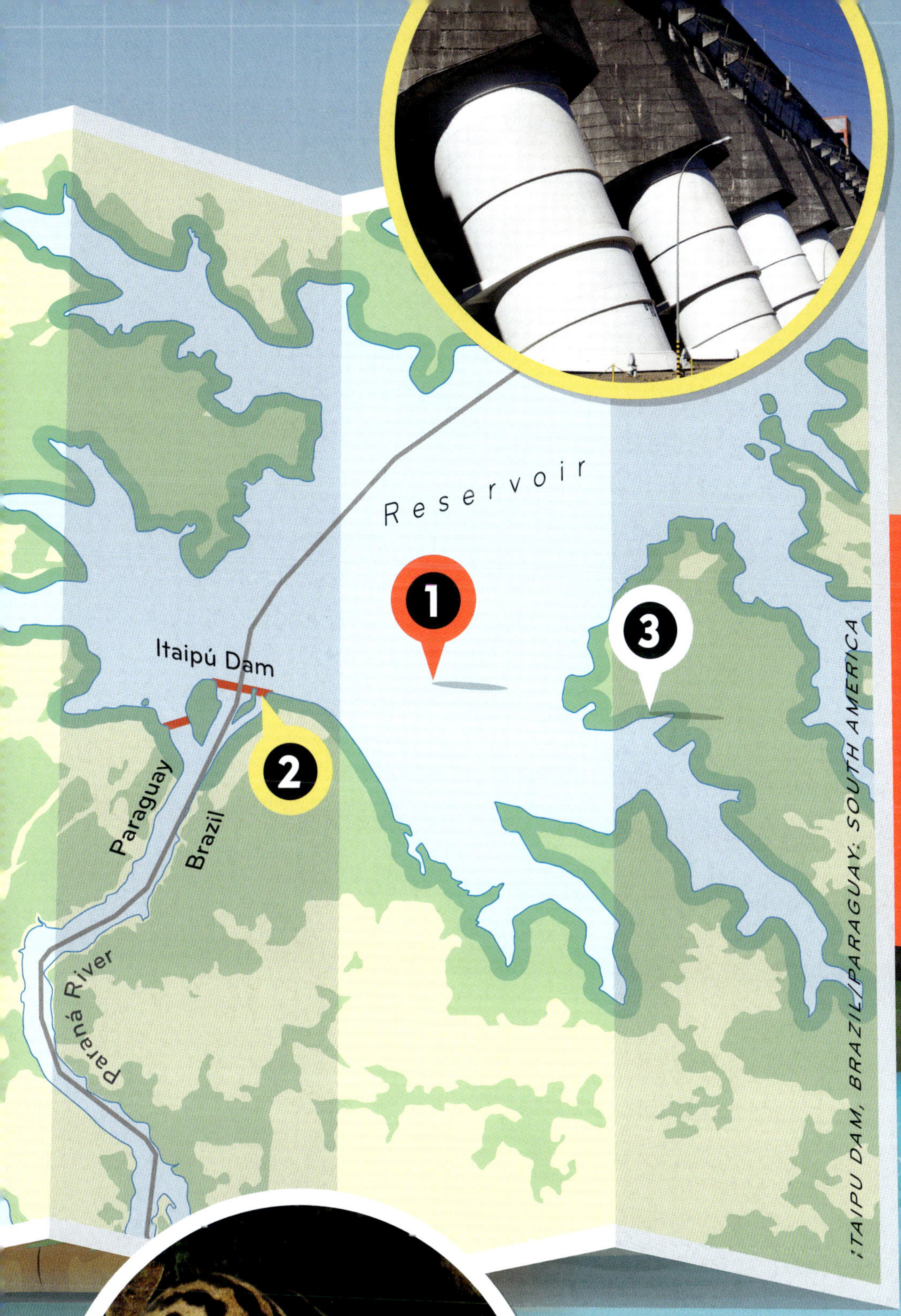

THE DAM

The Itaipú Dam has 20 massive turbine generators. It is hollow, a design used because it uses less concrete in building. Inside the dam, there is enough iron and steel to build 380 Eiffel Towers.

FACT

IN 2016, THE DAM PRODUCED 103.1 MILLION MWH POWER - TO PRODUCE THE SAME AS AN OIL-FUELED POWER PLANT YOU WOULD NEED 583,000 BARRELS OF OIL PER DAY!

THE ENVIRONMENT

There has been an environmental cost to building the Itaipú Dam. Creating the reservoir above it flooded land rich in plants and wildlife, and forced people to move. Production of concrete and metal is harmful to the environment. Today, an area has been established around the dam to protect wildlife.

GLOSSARY

antibiotics medicines given to people or animals to fight off infections

biodiversity the many different types of plants and animals that grow in one area

biomass organic matter used to produce energy

carbon dioxide a gas made when things are burned and which people and animals breathe out

climate change the rising temperature of the Earth's surface and its effects, such as melting ice caps and more extreme weather

concrete a substance used in building. It is very durable and when poured into a mold will harden to keep the set shape.

coniferous trees that produce cones and have needle-like leaves. They are usually evergreen and do not drop their leaves in winter.

delta a triangular area of land where a river divides into many smaller streams as it runs to the sea

ecosystem living things that exist together within a set environment

extract to take one substance out of a mixture

fertilizer a substance that can be added to soil to give nutrients for plants

livelihood a job or way of earning money needed to live on

orbit to move around something in a curved path. The planets orbit the sun.

organic made from once-living matter

pesticide chemicals used to kill pests that damage crops

pollution a substance or other waste that harms or damages the environment

prehistoric living before written history began

sub-Saharan a region in Africa south of the Sahara desert

turbine a machine designed to generate power by turning a wheel or rotor

FURTHER INFORMATION

Books

Earth's Resources (Fact Planet) by Izzi Howell (Franklin Watts, 2020)

Natural Resources (EcoGraphics) by Izzi Howell (Franklin Watts, 2019)

Source to Resource series by Michael Bright (Wayland, 2016)

The Incredible Ecosystems of Planet Earth by Rachel Ignotofsky (Wren & Rook, 2019)

Websites

www.bbc.co.uk/bitesize/topics/zshp34j/articles/z62qy9q

There's great information on the BBC Bitesize website.

foodmiles.com

Use the food miles website to track how far your food has traveled.

www.nationalgeographic.org/education/resource-library

Take a look at the Resource Library from National Geographic for information on everything Planet Earth!

INDEX